THE MINDFUL PILGRIMAGE

A 40-DAY POCKET DEVOTIONAL FOR PILGRIMS OF ANY FAITH OR NONE

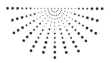

JEANETTE BANASHAK

DEDICATION
"For Beth, my pilgrim-partner"

Apocryphile Press
1700 Shattuck Ave. #81
Berkeley, CA 94709

CONTENTS

INTRODUCTION

This book is for people of any spiritual/religious/ethical tradition, or no tradition, who are about to begin a pilgrimage. The pilgrimage may be to The Camino of Santiago de Campostela, Shikoku, Mecca, Israel, India, Machu Picchu, the mountains, the sea, or anywhere else in the world that calls to you. The journey may also take you to your own home, where you might have set up sacred time and space to explore your inner landscape. Wherever you may be in this moment, you join thousands of other pilgrims who have gathered courage, resilience, and hope and are ready to take the first step into the unfolding universe ahead.

The book offers forty quotes from fellow sojourners. You will read from a variety of voices across centuries, religions, and cultures. Each quote does not stand alone, but is a part of a larger conversation. After each quote there are three questions that deal with the past, present, and future. They are intended to facilitate reflection of past experiences and relationships, provide grounding for the place you are at at the time, and offer prompts for future change.

The book is set up for you to read and reflect on with each new day of your pilgrimage. Trust that the words on the page are the words you need at the moment, and use them as points to ponder as you take each step. At the end of the day, you may want to go back and re-read the quotes or contemplate more deeply your responses to the words or the questions.

The number forty seems to be shorthand for "a long time." It has great significance in Judaism, Christianity, and Islam as a standard for deep transformation. In Judaism it represents transition, change, newness, trial, and repair. In Christianity, it represents reflection and preparation. In Islam, forty represents a time of waiting and anticipation. In Numerology, the number forty represents energy, the big picture, order, and building a solid foundation.

———

Before beginning, I want to ask you the following questions: What are you seeking? How do you believe this pilgrimage will help? What intention do you bring to the journey? What do you need to release? What do you need to hold/grasp/claim?

———

Go gently and with peace.

DAY 1: PILGRIMAGE

*P*eregrinatio is almost untranslatable, but its essence is caught in the ninth-century story of three Irishmen drifting over the sea from Ireland for seven days, in coracles without oars, coming ashore in Cornwall and then being brought to the court of King Alfred. When he asked them where they had come from and where they were going they answered that they "stole away because we wanted for the love of God to be on pilgrimage, we cared not where."

—Esther de Waal, *The Celtic Way of Prayer: The Recovery of the Religious Imagination*

---

1. Before you decided to do this pilgrimage, where were you going?
2. Does the Celtic understanding of *Peregrinatio* clarify what you may be seeking today?
3. How might you live each day as a pilgrim once home?

DAY 2: POSSIBILITIES

*T*he soul needs love as urgently as the body needs air. In the warmth of love, the soul can be itself. All the possibilities of your human destiny are asleep in your soul. You are here to realize and honor these possibilities. When love comes into your life, unrecognized dimensions of your destiny awaken and blossom and grow. Possibility is the secret heart of time.

—John O'Donohue, *Anam Cara*

1. What are some ways in which you have been asleep?
2. What is awakening in you today?
3. How has love come into your life on this pilgrimage? Who will you take with you as you journey on?

DAY 3: ALIVE

*P*eople say that what we're all seeking is a meaning for life. I don't think that's what we're really seeking. I think that what we're seeking is an experience of being alive, so that our life experiences on the purely physical plane will have resonances with our own innermost being and reality, so that we actually feel the rapture of being alive.

—Joseph Campbell, *The Power of Myth*

1. When have you felt a resonance between your outer life and inner life?
2. How alive do you feel right now? What is something you could do on your journey today to tune in to your aliveness?
3. What are some experiences of being alive you hope to have in the future?

DAY 4: BEGINNING

The pilgrimage does not begin with the first step or ride down the trail. Pilgrims begin to shape their journeys well before they leave the front door. The physical movement of arriving at the Camino is anticipated by some kind of internal movement—a decision, an impulse, an unexplained prompting, a long-held desire finally realized, a promise seeking fulfillment, a hope for change. The internal space is in some way already in flux before the journey begins—anticipatory, eager, confused, exhausted, open.

—Nancy Louise Frey, *Pilgrim Stories: On and Off the Road to Santiago*

---

1. What was the internal movement that compelled you to begin the Camino in the first place?
2. What is the internal movement that compels you to continue the Camino today?
3. Where will your internal space be when you end the journey?

DAY 5: SELF

*L*ife is cooking us, and we resist because we don't know our purpose in life, the "meal" that is being prepared. The cook says to the chickpeas, "You were once drinking fresh dew in the garden." That was so you could be a nice meal for the Guest. Don't dwell on the self you think you are. Let yourself be transformed into something even better—a meal for the Beloved. In Rumi's view, the whole universe is involved in transformation, in eating and being eaten for the sake of an evolution driven by love. Perhaps life is showing you right now a face of the Beloved reflected somewhere within, which feels greater than your small self or any part of it, and you cannot deny it. Or, you are calling to the place deep within you that is ready to manifest this face in yourself.

—Neil Douglas-Klotz, *The Sufi Book of Life: 99 Pathways of the Heart for the Modern Dervish*

---

1. What have you been resisting because of not knowing the purpose?

2. What does the face of the Beloved reflected within look like today?

3. How will this pilgrimage help you to call to the place deep within you in the coming months?

DAY 6: REWARD

*W*hen we want something, we have to have a clear purpose in mind for the thing that we want. The only reason for seeking a reward is to know what to do with that reward.

—Paulo Coelho, *The Pilgrimage*

---

1. Have you sought a reward—something that is given in return for good or evil done or received—in the past? And did you know what to do with it once you received it?
2. What is your reason today for taking this pilgrimage?
3. What reward will this pilgrimage bring to you? To those with whom you live and work?

DAY 7: ATTENTION

One day a man of the people said to Zen Master Ikkyu: "Master, will you please write for me some maxims of the highest wisdom?" Ikkyu immediately took his brush and wrote the word "Attention." "Is that all?" asked the man. "Will you not add something more?" Ikkyu then wrote twice running: "Attention. Attention." "Well," remarked the man rather irritably, "I really don't see much depth or subtlety in what you have just written." Then Ikkyu wrote the same word three times running: "Attention. Attention. Attention." Half angered, the man demanded: "What does that word 'Attention' mean anyway?" And Ikkyu answered gently: "Attention means attention."

—Roshi P. Kapleau, *The Three Pillars of Zen*

1. Where in your life have you been inattentive?
2. What is the one thing you need to attend to today?
3. How do you anticipate your growth in attention extending into your life after the pilgrimage?

DAY 8: GLORY

$\mathcal{R}$emember that you have only one soul; that you have only one death to die; that you have only one life, which is short and has to be lived by you alone; and there is only one Glory, which is eternal. If you do this, there will be many things about which you care nothing.

—St. Teresa of Ávila, *The Way of Perfection: The Maxims and Counsels Given to Her Sisters in Religion*

1. What are some things you have cared about too much in the past year?
2. What are the things that you care about today as you begin your journey?
3. Do you have any plans to give up anything once the pilgrimage is complete? What is it?

DAY 9: STORY LINE

$\mathcal{U}$sually we regard loneliness as an enemy. Heartache is not something we choose to invite in. It's restless and pregnant and hot with the desire to escape and find something or someone to keep us company. When we can rest in the middle, we begin to have a nonthreatening relationship with loneliness, a relaxing and cooling loneliness that completely turns our usual fearful patterns upside down... After we practice less desire wholeheartedly and consistently, something shifts. We feel less desire in the sense of being less solidly seduced by our Very Important Story Lines. So even if the hot loneliness is there, and for 1.6 seconds we sit with that restlessness when yesterday we couldn't sit for even one, that's the journey of the warrior.

—Pema Chödrön, *When Things Fall Apart: Heart Advice For Difficult Times*

---

1. What has your experience with loneliness been like throughout your life?

2. How would you like to befriend your loneliness today?
3. How might you change your Story Line as you work with your desires?

DAY 10: THE WAY

The Way is how the wise become wise. The Way is not a fixed set of disciplines, prescriptions, commandments, or laws. The Way is more strategy than tactics... The Way is not a particular way—a way that can be packaged, sold, and followed as one might follow a recipe to bake a cake. Rather, the Way is your way, the way you find useful for awakening to the Truth manifesting in you, with you, and around you here and now... The Way *to* Truth is the Way *of* Truth; you do not arrive at the kingdom of heaven but rather live the kingdom of heaven wherever you happen to be at this and every moment: "God is with you wherever you are" (Qur'an 57:4).

—Rami Shapiro, *The World Wisdom Bible: A New Testament for a Global Spirituality*

---

1. How have you lived the Way in your life? What are some points in time where you were living the Way of Truth?

2. If you were to transform your consciousness today, what in your life might become aligned?
3. What will your pursuit of the Way look like upon finishing your journey?

DAY 11: SUMMIT

*Y*ou cannot stay on the summit forever; you have to come down again. So why bother in the first place? Just this: What is above knows what is below, but what is below does not know what is above. One climbs, one sees. One descends, one sees no longer, but one has seen. There is an art of conducting oneself in the lower regions by the memory of what one saw higher up. When one can no longer see, one can at least still know.

—René Daumal, *Mount Analogue*

1. Is there something that you have not fully found freedom from or in from your past? Is there a ritual or ceremony that you would like to perform today to move forward?
2. How will you take what you've seen on the pilgrimage and include it in your conscious choices today?
3. How will you conduct yourself differently at home because of what you've seen?

DAY 12: HAPPINESS

To gain experience in the profound teachings brings happiness.
To gain no experience at all brings happiness...
To stay in retreat in the mountains brings happiness...
To eat the food of great bliss brings happiness.
To wear the clothes of luminosity brings happiness.
To practice the path of the messenger brings happiness.
To keep one's focus at the tip of the nose brings happiness.
—*Siddha Advayavajra, From* Timeless Rapture: Inspired Verse of the Shangpa Masters, *compiled by Jamgon Kongtrul, trans. & ed. by Ngawang Zangpo.*

1. What has brought you happiness in your life?
2. If you were to write your own song or poem or story about happiness, what would it say today?
3. When you have completed the journey, is there anything you would like to change in your life to bring you true happiness?

DAY 13: EXPLORATION

When you give yourself to places, they give you yourself back; the more one comes to know them, the more one seeds them with the invisible crop of memories and associations that will be waiting for you when you come back, while new places offer up new thoughts, new possibilities. Exploring the world is one of the best ways of exploring the mind and walking travels both terrains.

—Rebecca Solnit, *Wanderlust: A History of Walking*

---

1. What are some of the journeys you have taken that have provided new insight to you?
2. What aspects of your heart, mind, body, and spirit are you exploring today?
3. What places in the future do you hope to explore and get to know? What draws you to them?

DAY 14: CHOICE

*T*o know God, you must consciously participate in making this journey—that is the purpose of free will. On the surface of life we make much more trivial choices, but pretend that they carry enormous weight. In reality, you are constantly acting out seven fundamental choices about the kind of world you recognize:

The choice of fear if you want to struggle and barely survive.

The choice of power if you want to compete and achieve.

The choice of inner reflection if you want peace.

The choice to know yourself if you want insight.

The choice to create if you want to discover the workings of nature.

The choice to love if you want to heal others and yourself.

The choice to be if you want to appreciate the infinite scope of God's creation.

—Deepak Chopra, *How to Know God: The Soul's Journey Into the Mystery*

1. When and why have you chosen fear or power in your life?
2. Which choice do you make today? What/who is compelling you to make that choice?
3. How will you change your pattern of choosing in the future?

DAY 15: DETAILS

*I*t is those who have a deep and real inner life who are best able to deal with the irritating details of outer life.
—Evelyn Underhill, in Annice Callahan's *Evelyn Underhill: Spirituality for Daily Living*

1. How would you describe your inner and outer life before this pilgrimage?
2. What are the quotidian details of today that point you to the Divine?
3. How will this journey have a lasting impact on your life?

DAY 16: TREE

Sometimes I came across a tree which seemed like a Buddha or a Jesus: Loving, compassionate, still, unambitious, enlightened, in eternal meditation, giving pleasure to a pilgrim, shade to a cow, berries to a bird, beauty to its surroundings, health to its neighbors, branches for the fire, leaves for the soil, asking nothing in return, in total harmony with the wind and the rain. How much can I learn from a tree? The tree is my church, the tree is my temple, the tree is my mantra, the tree is my poem and my prayer.

—Satish Kumar, *No Destination*

1. What is something in nature that you have learned from? Why do you think it resonated with you at that time?
2. What is like a tree for you on this path? Add a few more images to Kumar's description of the tree. The tree is…
3. What else would you like to learn from a tree?

DAY 17: FUEL

*W*e are simultaneously matter and spirit. In order to understand ourselves and be healthy in both body and spirit, we have to understand how matter and spirit interact, what draws the spirit of life force out of our bodies, and how we can retrieve our spirits from the false gods of fear, anger, and attachments to the past. Every attachment we hold on to out of fear commands a circuit of our spirit to leave our energy field and, to use a biblical phrase, "breathe life onto earth"—earth that costs us health. What drains your spirit drains your body. What fuels your spirit fuels your body. The power that fuels our bodies, our minds, and our hearts does not originate in our DNA. Rather, it has roots in Divinity itself.

—Caroline Myss, *Anatomy of the Spirit: The Seven Stages of Power and Healing*

1. What are some attachments you have held onto resulting in life force being drawn out of you?

2. What is something from the past that you need to let go of in order to be present today? Take some time, if needed, to do that.

3. What will fuel your spirit and body once you've completed the journey?

DAY 18: MEANING

*I*t is not so much the meaning of life that we seek, but our aliveness. When we have that, the meaning of life is obvious.

—Anodea Judith, *Eastern Body, Western Mind*

---

1. Have you had any experiences with energy release that was once blocked in your body? Describe the sensations.
2. What is the meaning of life for you today?
3. How will you pursue being alive once you complete this pilgrimage?

DAY 19: ORDINARY & UNIQUE

$\mathcal{H}$e had learned that it was the smallness of people that filled him with wonder and tenderness, and the loneliness of that too. The world was made up of people putting one foot in front of the other; and a life might appear ordinary simply because the person living it had been doing it for a long time. Harold could no longer pass a stranger without acknowledging the truth that everyone was the same, and also unique; and that this was the dilemma of being human.

—Rachel Joyce, *The Unlikely Pilgrimage of Harold Fry*

---

1. How ordinary was your life before you began the pilgrimage?
2. When you pass a stranger today, what ordinary things will you look for? What unique things?
3. Name a few ways that you would like to live as both an ordinary and unique person in the future.

DAY 20: WORK

*T*he busiest people I have known in my life always have time enough to do everything. Those who do nothing are always tired and pay no attention to the little amount of work they are required to do. They complain constantly that the day is too short. The truth is, they are afraid to fight the good fight.

—Paulo Coelho, *The Pilgrimage*

1. When have you felt as though the days were too short?
2. What is the good fight that you are taking on today?
3. How do you plan to make time for the things that matter to you when you have completed the pilgrimage?

DAY 21: GARDEN

*A*lmost from the beginning of my sentence on Robben Island, I asked the authorities for permission to start a garden in the courtyard. For years they refused without a reason. But eventually they relented, and we were able to cut a small garden on a narrow patch of earth against the far wall... A garden was one of the few things in prison that one could control. To plant a seed, watch it grow, to tend it and then harvest it, offered a simple but enduring satisfaction. The sense of being the custodian of this small patch of earth offered a small taste of freedom.

—Nelson Mandela, *Long Walk to Freedom*

1. Nelson Mandela is writing about a literal garden, but there are other levels of interpretation we can explore. Seeing the garden as your life, what were some of the ways you tended to your life in order to get to the point of taking the pilgrimage?
2. What aspect of your life today would you like to tend

to? Once the day is done, make sure you experience the satisfaction that comes with the cultivation.

3. Are there any parts of your life that you would like to tend to when the pilgrimage is completed? What are they?

DAY 22: NOURISHMENT

*W*hat is it you want to change? Your hair, your face, your body? Why? For God is in love with all those things and might weep when they are gone.

—St. Catherine of Siena, translated by Daniel Ladinsky in *Love Poems From God*

---

1. What was your relationship with your body as you were growing up? What were some of the cultural voices that influenced you, or not?
2. What is your relationship to your body today? What can you say to your body to nourish it?
3. What are some of the habits around nourishment (spiritual, emotional, physical, mental, etc.) that you would like to cultivate once you are back home?

DAY 23: EVERYWHERE

*E*verything is an avenue leading to the experience of Ultimate Reality. The divine communicates itself in all things. There are infinite ways to encounter the source. Ultimate Reality may be experienced in virtually anything. There is no place, no activity that restricts the divine. It is everywhere.

—Br. Wayne Teasdale, *A Monk in the World*

1. What is one of the most profound encounters that you have had with Ultimate Reality?
2. Look around you now, listen to your surroundings. Where is the Divine?
3. Where will you look and/or listen for Ultimate Reality upon completion of your journey?

DAY 24: PRAYER

That prayer has great power which a person makes with all their might. It makes a sour heart sweet, a sad heart merry, a poor heart rich, a foolish heart wise, a timid heart brave, a sick heart well, a blind heart full of sight, a cold heart ardent. It draws down the great God into the little heart; it drives the hungry soul up into the fullness of God; it brings together two lovers, God and the soul, in a wondrous place where they speak much of love.

—Mechthild of Magdeburg, *Mechthild of Magdeburg: The Flowing Light of the Godhead: The Revelations of Mechthild of Magdeburg*

---

1. How would you describe your prayer life before your pilgrimage?
2. How would you describe your heart today?
3. What would it be like for your soul to be swept up into the fullness of God? Of what love would you speak?

DAY 25: PEACE

*P*eace is present right here and now, in ourselves and in everything we do and see. Every breath we take, every step we take, can be filled with peace, joy, and serenity. The question is whether or not we are in touch with it. We need only to be awake, alive in the present moment.

—Thich Nhat Hanh, *Peace Is Every Step: The Path of Mindfulness in Everyday Life*

1. When was the last time you experienced a deep sense of peace? How did it feel to be that peaceful?
2. How awake are you today to be filled with peace, joy, and serenity? How can you spend some time taking some deep breaths and getting in touch with this part of you?
3. How will you continue to pursue peace tomorrow and the day after tomorrow and the day after that?

DAY 26: ATTITUDE

*A*ll Birds find shelter during a rain. But Eagle avoids rain by flying above the Clouds. Problems are common, but attitude makes the difference!!!

—Abdul Kalam, *Wings of Fire: An Autobiography of APJ Abdul Kalam*

---

1. Have you been a person who finds shelter during a storm? Have you avoided the rain by flying above the clouds? Think about some of the instances when times have been difficult.
2. If you could put an image to your attitude today, what would it be?
3. When times are tough, what are the ways in which you will fly above the clouds?

DAY 27: OUR WORLD

e cannot live in a world that is not our own, in a world that is interpreted for us by others. An interpreted world is not a home. Part of the terror is to take back our own listening, to use our own voice, to see our own light.
—Hildegard of Bingen

1. How have you lived by others' rules, others' interpretations, or others' worldviews?
2. How has this current journey helped you to take back your own listening, use your own voice, or see your own light?
3. How could you share that with others? How might you do that once you have completed the pilgrimage?

DAY 28: GROWING

*W*hat moves us from one level to another? That is the question… We just keep listening, growing in trust, and growing in love… As we journey more deeply inward… its effects lead us powerfully outward, toward… the capacity to relate to one another with the unconditional love with which Christ relates to us.

—Thomas Keating, *Intimacy With God*

1. As you think about your spiritual journey thus far, when have you moved from one level to another?
2. What do you long for today as you journey inward? Outward?
3. Once completed with this journey, what do you hope will be different about the way you relate to others? Yourself? The Divine?

DAY 29: LAND

*L*istening to the land is a practice of healing and balance for us as humans. It is listening to the whole body, which is none other than the whole world. This practice involves taking time to be with ourselves, and to listen to what our bodies are saying. We all know the major signs with which our bodies speak to us, such as hunger, thirst, fatigue, stress, and pleasure. But there are also more subtle messages from our bodies: discomfort, unease, peacefulness, and relaxation. An integral aspect of this practice is turning inward to ourselves, quieting down the outer and inner chatter, and attending to our inner experience.

—Michael S. Hutton, *Listening to the Land* in Mark Brady's *The Wisdom of Listening*

---

1. What experiences have you had listening to the land? How did your body help or hinder that listening?
2. What might be hindering your inner experience today?

3. What aspect of the land, the world, your body, do you hope to listen to more deeply for the remainder of your pilgrimage?

DAY 30: HEART

The greatest challenge of the day is: how to bring about a revolution of the heart, a revolution which has to start with each one of us? When we begin to take the lowest place, to wash the feet of others, to love our brothers [*sic*] with that burning love, that passion, which led to the Cross, then we can truly say, "Now I have begun."

—Dorothy Day, *Loaves and Fishes*

1. What was the revolution of your heart that prompted you to take this journey?
2. What does it mean for you to take "the lowest place" today?
3. What will this revolution of the heart look like once you return to the ordinary life?

DAY 31: RITUAL

I am convinced that pilgrimage is still a bona fide spirit-renewing ritual. But I also believe in pilgrimage as a powerful metaphor for *any* journey with the purpose of finding something that matters deeply to the traveler. With a deepening focus, keen preparation, attention to the path below our feet, and respect for the destination at hand, it is possible to transform even the most ordinary trip into a sacred journey, a pilgrimage… What legendary travelers have taught us since Pausanias and Marco Polo is that the art of travel is the art of seeing what is sacred. Pilgrimage is the kind of journeying that marks just this move from mindless to mindful, soulless to soulful travel.

—Phil Cousineau, *The Art of Pilgrimage: The Seeker's Guide to Making Travel Sacred*

1. When have you engaged in mindless or soulless travel?
2. What are you seeing today that is sacred?
3. What can you do to travel mindfully and soulfully in your daily life?

DAY 32: SOUL

*Y*ou are in my soul, completely You
have entered me... a friend is
meant
be such a one; and so it's about You
if I talk, for You I yearn when
silent
—Ra'bia of Basra, *Ra'bia of Basra: Selected Poems*

---

1. What metaphors for the Divine have you used in
   the past?
2. What metaphor for the Divine will you contemplate
   today?
3. How do you anticipate creating space for the Divine
   and for silence at the end of your journey and back to
   the ordinary world?

DAY 33: FAITH

*a*n authentic spiritual meltdown is a cause for celebration. It is only then that we are stripped of our attachment to the way the presence of God is supposed to feel, and begin to rest in spiritual nakedness. Divested of our constructs about the existence and nature of this God, we come face to face with Ultimate Reality. In the midst of our crumbling, we may not see it as grace. In fact, it looks as though we are giving up on God or, even worse, that God has abandoned us.

—Mirabai Starr, *God of Love*

1. When have you felt abandoned by God or as though you had given up on God?
2. What difficulty are you struggling with on this journey that, with a subtle shift in energy, you might see as grace?
3. What will you want to remember about your physical journey? Why is it so significant to your spiritual journey?

DAY 34: PRESENT

The most important hour is always the present.

The most significant person is precisely the one sitting across from you right now.

The most necessary work is always love.

—Meister Eckhart, *The Complete Mystical Works of Meister Eckhart*

---

1. What has been the most important hour, the most significant person, the most necessary work for you in the past?
2. How will you be present to every hour and every person you encounter today?
3. What work do you still need to do on loving well?

DAY 35: MOUNTAINS

*B*efore a man studies Zen, to him mountains are mountains and waters are waters; after he gets an insight into the truth of Zen through the instruction of a good master, mountains to him are not mountains and waters are not waters; but after this, when he really attains to the abode of rest, mountains are once more mountains and waters are waters.

—Seigen Ishin, in D.T. Suzuki's *Essays in Zen Buddhism*

1. Who has been an instructor for you in your faith?
2. What truth do the mountains reveal to you today?
3. Once completed with the journey, how will you remain open and receptive to what the universe uncovers for you?

DAY 36: INTUITION

*L*et us introduce you to the guide to this inner journey: your Intuitive Consciousness. This guide has always been there, although you may not have been aware of its existence and its inherent wisdom. It is like the Roman god Mercury, who mediates between heaven and earth. As we progress along the path we get to know this guide more intimately; the tone of its voice, the feel of its presence, the comfort of its steady watching, the wisdom of its insight and clear unwavering waymarks.

For some, it sounds like a still wise voice from the heart that arises in us as a thought or insight; in other moments it is present as a felt sense, or appears as images, uninfluenced by one-sided judgments and polarities. Intuitive Consciousness may manifest as a sudden flash of intuition in a creative moment. Once we follow the path of this guide it watches over us like the steady reassuring presence of a guardian angel.

—Sara Hollwey & Jill Brierly, *The Inner Camino: A Path of Awakening*

1. What kind of relationship have you had with your intuitive consciousness?
2. What voice, thought, insight, presence, or image is coming to you today?
3. What will your response be to Intuitive Consciousness if she invites you to follow a path that involves change?

DAY 37: MISSION

$\mathcal{F}$or our own good, each of us needs to learn what our
mission is, because the details of how we live our
lives accumulate to create health or illness... the little troubles
and major traumas that we go through take up residence and live
in our bodies and affect or block our energy... By coming to
know your mission, you can live your life in a way that makes
best use of your energy. When you are working well with your
energy, you are also making the best expression of your personal
power. I call this living in accord with your Sacred Contract.

—Caroline Myss, *Sacred Contracts*

1. Have you been accumulating healthier illness in your
   body? Where has your energy been blocked?
2. How would you articulate your personal mission?
   What is something you can do today to bring your
   personal power and your energy together?
3. How much are you willing to surrender comfort,
   security, control, or approval to fulfill your mission?

DAY 38: THOUGHTS

*T*houghts are like the breeze or the leaves on the trees or the raindrops falling. They appear like that, and through inquiry we can make friends with them. Would you argue with a raindrop? Raindrops aren't personal, and neither are thoughts. Once a painful concept is met with understanding, the next time it appears you may find it interesting. What used to be the nightmare is now just interesting. The next time it appears, you may find it funny. The next time, you may not even notice it. This is the power of loving what is.

—Byron Katie, *Loving What Is: Four Questions That Can Change Your Life*

---

1. What are some thoughts that used to be nightmares for you?
2. What are some thoughts today you could befriend and meet with understanding and compassion?
3. What will you do when you catch yourself attaching to or avoiding thoughts?

DAY 39: WELLSPRING

*W*hat we all need to do is find the wellspring that keeps us going, that gives us the strength and patience to keep up this struggle for a long time.
—Winona LaDuke

---

1. How have you cultivated strength and patience in your life?
2. What or who is the wellspring that sustains you today?
3. What causes or struggles will you fight for when you complete your journey?

DAY 40: COURAGE

*T*his unsettling time is a good time to *take courage*, to set out as pilgrims to rediscover the sacredness of this earth and her peoples, to immerse ourselves in travel on some hallowed Way, not with trepidation but with derring-do, stepping lightly and "finding every stone in the road precious." This risk takes courage. Risk is the warp upon which pilgrim spirit is woven. The woof is time. The journey, the actual setting out and traveling to a hallowed site, even in a journey of memories, is the loom upon which all is fixed. The ongoing pattern, hue and texture, is life itself.

—Rosanne Keller, *Pilgrim in Time: Mindful Journeys to Encounter the Sacred*

---

1. What felt like the biggest (or one of the biggest) risks you took during this journey? Do you know why it loomed so large?
2. How would you describe your pilgrim spirit today?

How is your spirit influencing your attitude and what you celebrate?

3. What is one risk that you would like to take back home in ordinary time?

AFTERWORD

What are the stories you don't want to ever forget from your pilgrimage? Who did you meet along the way and what attracted you or repelled you from them? How did you meet yourself in new ways? What are some of the snapshots that you will replay repeatedly? In this moment, how would you describe some of the ways you may have changed during the course of your pilgrimage? What does life expect of you now that you've completed the journey?

Learning theory suggests that we remember best what we learned in the beginnings and ends of things. What details from your first days on the pilgrimage do you remember? My hope is that this book will serve as a reminder of what you were thinking and feeling during the space in between, as well as how you commenced and completed your pilgrimage. Perhaps you have left behind or let go of old and outdated ideologies, relationships, or habits. In their place, you have been invited to new awareness, developed deeper connection with self and others, and committed to healthy practices.

Through time, you will organize and interpret your experiences and find meaning in your encounters. You may find that as you continue to become more authentically you, the meanings of your experiences change. You may ascribe personal meaning to your experiences, or understand a completely (or subtly) different way of *being* altogether. Perhaps you find yourself more courageous in the face of fear. Or, perhaps you feel activated to pursue justice from a contemplative posture. Or, maybe you have accessed a gentle and loving source of life inside of you that serves as a compass for making decisions.

Because you joined countless others through history, your pilgrimage was an immersion into what Br. Wayne Teasdale called the *mystic heart.* It transcended the borders of religions and led you to an interconnected space where all our hearts unite. The journey is never over, though our state of being home gets intensified as we become more conscious of the moment and of our universal core experiences of being human.

You, dear pilgrims, are our heroes. Thank you for responding to the nudge that prompted you to endeavor such a pilgrimage.

Printed in Great Britain
by Amazon

46248112R00037